In the Beginning

A Month of Daily
Meditations from

Al-Taurat

You can contact the author at: yaqubduncan@yahoo.co.uk

Cover Design: Innovivid, info@innovivid.co.uk
Project Directed by: Tooth Design & Print Consultants, andi@atconsultants.co.uk
Printing: Knox Press

Cover Photo: Sunrise from Mount Sinai where Propher Musa received revelation from Allah

In the Name of Allah, Most Gracious,
Most Merciful

Introduction

Where have we come from? This is the question of origins. It is asked by people everywhere in the world. Al-Taurat takes us back to the beginning of all things. It tells us where we have come from and how we originated. Al-Taurat introduces us to Allah, the Creator of all things. Al-Taurat goes on to tell us who we are as human beings, and why we are here. It also tells us what is wrong with our world and why. What matters could be more important than these?

The first book in al-Taurat is called in English, "Genesis", which means origins. This book you are now reading looks at the opening three chapters of Genesis. It is divided into thirty days of readings. For each day there is a section of the text printed as originally revealed by Allah in the Hebrew language. There is then a translation by the author into English. This is followed by a brief meditation on the reading from al-Taurat. At the end of each day there is a du'a of response[1].

Al-Taurat – a Holy Book

Muslims, Christians and Jews all recognise Al-Taurat as a holy book which was revealed to the Prophet Musa[2]. It forms the first part of the Kitab-i-Muqaddas or Holy Bible. It is made up of five books, known in English as Genesis, Exodus, Leviticus, Numbers and Deuteronomy.

But do we still have the original Taurat? Has it not been changed? All the evidence shows that we do still have the original available to us. Jews and Christians have exactly the same Taurat. One or the other community could not possibly have changed it, because then they would have different books. The Qur'an also testifies about al-Taurat:

Say: "We believe in Allah, and in what has been revealed to us and

---

[1] Due to limitations of space, quotations from the Taurat, Zabur, Injil or Qur'an in the mediation section are in English translation only.

[2] This book does not follow the practice of placing a phrase after a prophet's name such as, 'peace be upon him.' However, this should not be viewed as showing a lack of respect for Allah's prophets, whom the author holds in high honour.

what was revealed to Abraham, Ishmael; Isaac, Jacob, and the tribes, and in (the Books) given to Moses, Jesus and the prophets from their Lord" (al-'Imran 3:84).

It is He who sent down to you (step by step), in truth, the book, confirming what went before it; and He sent down the Law (of Moses) and the Gospel (of Jesus)[3] (al-'Imran 3:3).

There are copies of al-Taurat that are dated centuries before the Muslim era. Among the Dead Sea Scrolls were copies of parts of al-Taurat which were from before the Christian era. This proves that al-Taurat could not have been changed after the time of the Prophet Muhammad. From an Islamic perspective, al-Taurat could not have been changed before the Qur'an was given. How could the Qur'an confirm something that was corrupt?

Allah's Word lasts forever
In addition, Taurat, Zabur, Injil and Qur'an all agree that Allah's words last forever and cannot be destroyed or altered:

Your word, O LORD, is eternal; it stands firm in the heavens. (Zabur 119:89)[4]

The word of our God stands forever. (Isaiah 40:8)

It is easier for heaven and earth to disappear than for the least stroke of a pen to drop out of al-Taurat. (Injil, Luke 16:17)

There is none that can alter the words of Allah. (Qur'an, al-An'am 6:34)[5]

Thus, we can be certain that the text of al-Taurat in the Hebrew language

---

[3] In English, Taurat is 'Law', Zabur is 'Psalms' and Injil is 'Gospel.'

[4] This means the Zabur, chapter 119, verse 89. The numbers written in small letters in the English translations of al-Taurat are the verse or ayah numbers. Sometimes references are given in the meditation or prayer section, eg. "v.1-3"; this means that it is referring to verses 1 to 3, or "1:31" which means chapter 1 verse 31.

which we possess today is that originally given by Allah. Therefore, we should revere al-Taurat as the very words of Allah. We should read and study it and seek to submit our lives to it.

This book comes to you with the prayer that Allah may bless you greatly through reading and studying His Word.

Ya'qub Duncan

---

[5]Quotations from the Qur'an are from: "The Meaning of the Holy Qur'an – English Translation by Abdullah Yusuf Ali, New Modern English Edition." Quotations from the Taurat, Zabur and Injil are from: "The Holy Bible, Today's New International Version" (Some English names are substituted with names more familiar to Muslims).

Du'a

"Teach me LORD, the way of Your decrees, that I may follow it to the end. Give me understanding, so that I may keep Your Taurat and obey it with all my heart."
(Zabur 119:33-34)

Day 1

Al-Taurat - Genesis 1:1-2

¹ בְּרֵאשִׁית בָּרָא אֱלֹהִים אֵת הַשָּׁמַיִם וְאֵת הָאָרֶץ׃ ² וְהָאָרֶץ הָיְתָה תֹהוּ וָבֹהוּ וְחֹשֶׁךְ עַל־פְּנֵי תְהוֹם וְרוּחַ אֱלֹהִים מְרַחֶפֶת עַל־פְּנֵי הַמָּיִם׃

¹In the beginning Allah created the heavens and the earth. ²Now the earth was formless and empty and darkness was over the surface of the deep. And the Spirit of Allah hovered over the surface of the waters.

The opening words of al-Taurat take us back to the very beginning of time, of history and of all things. It takes us to the point of origin. The term, "heavens and the earth" simply means the whole universe - every thing that exists. Allah created everything (see Qur'an, Ibrahim 14:32).

First of all, these opening words tell us about Allah (the word in the original Hebrew text is *Elohim*. This has the same root as the Arabic word, Allah). Allah was already there in the beginning. Allah Himself had no beginning. He always was. The universe had a beginning, but Allah is *al-Samad*, the eternal (see Qur'an, al-Ikhlas 112:2).

It is also very clear from these words and the whole of al-Taurat that Allah is *al-Ahad*, the One. "Hear O Isra'il, the LORD your Allah, the LORD is One" (al-Taurat – Deuteronomy 6:4).

Before the beginning, the universe did not exist. Allah created it out of nothing. How great and awesome is Allah!

When Allah created the earth, it was formless, empty and dark. It was waiting to be filled by Allah, according to His plan. Allah's Spirit hovered over the surface of the waters. This suggests that, although Allah is distinct and separate from His creation, He has a close concern for it and is deeply involved with it.

Du'a: "Before the mountains were born or you brought forth the earth and the world, from everlasting to everlasting you are Allah." (Zabur 90:2)

Day 2

Al-Taurat - Genesis 1:3-5

³ וַיֹּאמֶר אֱלֹהִים יְהִי אוֹר וַיְהִי־
אוֹר: ⁴ וַיַּרְא אֱלֹהִים אֶת־הָאוֹר כִּי־
טוֹב וַיַּבְדֵּל אֱלֹהִים בֵּין הָאוֹר
וּבֵין הַחֹשֶׁךְ: ⁵ וַיִּקְרָא אֱלֹהִים׀ לָאוֹר
יוֹם וְלַחֹשֶׁךְ קָרָא לָיְלָה וַיְהִי־עֶרֶב
וַיְהִי־בֹקֶר יוֹם אֶחָד:

³And Allah said, "Let there be light"
– and there was light. ⁴Allah saw the
light, that it was good. And Allah
separated the light from the darkness.
⁵Allah called the light "day", and the
darkness he called "night". And there
was evening and there was morning,
the first day.

In the events of the first day, there are a number of features that are repeated throughout the creation account.

"And Allah said..." Here we see Allah as a speaking Being. He talks, He communicates.

"Allah said, 'Let there be light,' and there was light." He speaks into the darkness and emptiness and light appears. Later on too, Allah speaks things into existence. We human beings can speak, but we can't speak things into existence. What amazing power belongs to Allah! He creates without effort. He is truly *al-Qahir*, the Almighty.

"Allah saw the light, that it was good." Allah surveys his work. He takes pleasure in it, perhaps like an artist who steps back to look at the work of art he has just produced. Allah appreciates all that is good and beautiful. All of Allah's creation is good. It reflects the goodness of the Creator.

Light is truly wonderful. Think of how the light changes all the time, the low lights of dawn and dusk, or the brilliance of the midday sun in summer, or the gentle light of a summer evening.

Du'a: I praise You, Allah, for the light; I praise You for the beauty and goodness of all You have made. I praise You that You are both almighty and absolutely good.

Day 3

Al-Taurat - Genesis 1:6-8

⁶ וַיֹּאמֶר אֱלֹהִים יְהִי רָקִיעַ בְּתוֹךְ הַמָּיִם
וִיהִי מַבְדִּיל בֵּין מַיִם לָמָיִם: ⁷ וַיַּעַשׂ
אֱלֹהִים אֶת־הָרָקִיעַ וַיַּבְדֵּל בֵּין הַמַּיִם
אֲשֶׁר מִתַּחַת לָרָקִיעַ וּבֵין הַמַּיִם אֲשֶׁר
מֵעַל לָרָקִיעַ וַיְהִי־כֵן: ⁸ וַיִּקְרָא אֱלֹהִים
לָרָקִיעַ שָׁמָיִם וַיְהִי־עֶרֶב וַיְהִי־בֹקֶר יוֹם
שֵׁנִי:

⁶And Allah said, "Let there be an expanse between the waters, and let it separate water from water. ⁷So Allah made the expanse and separated between the water which was under the expanse and the water which was above the expanse. And it was so. ⁸Allah called the expanse "sky". And there was evening and there was morning, the second day.

On day one of creation, Allah divided or separated light from darkness. Now He separates between the water below the sky (the sea), and the water above (probably clouds). Allah creates order out of chaos. He creates what are often called, "the laws of nature." Allah is the law-giver. Human science is the discovery and understanding of these laws. Science is only possible because Allah made the universe an ordered place.

"And it was so." Again we see the power of Allah's word. He speaks and things come into being

"And there was evening and there was morning, the second day." Al-Taurat presents Allah's creation in six days. The Qur'an does the same (al-A'raf 7:54, Hud 11:7, as-Sajdah 32:4). This could mean that creation happened in the space of a literal week, or it might be a literary device for presenting the completeness of Allah's creation. The main purpose of this chapter, is not so that we will know exactly how long it took for Allah to create the universe, but so that we might worship Him and give thanks.

Du'a: Allah, thank you for the order that You have made in creation. Thank you that creation follows Your laws. How they display Your wisdom! Help me to follow Your laws for humankind.

Day 4

Al-Taurat - Genesis 1:9-13

⁹ וַיֹּ֣אמֶר אֱלֹהִ֗ים יִקָּו֨וּ הַמַּ֜יִם מִתַּ֤חַת הַשָּׁמַ֙יִם֙ אֶל־מָק֣וֹם אֶחָ֔ד וְתֵרָאֶ֖ה הַיַּבָּשָׁ֑ה וַֽיְהִי־כֵֽן׃ ¹⁰ וַיִּקְרָ֨א אֱלֹהִ֤ים ׀ לַיַּבָּשָׁה֙ אֶ֔רֶץ וּלְמִקְוֵ֥ה הַמַּ֖יִם קָרָ֣א יַמִּ֑ים וַיַּ֥רְא אֱלֹהִ֖ים כִּי־טֽוֹב׃ ¹¹ וַיֹּ֣אמֶר אֱלֹהִ֗ים תַּֽדְשֵׁ֤א הָאָ֙רֶץ֙ דֶּ֗שֶׁא עֵ֚שֶׂב מַזְרִ֣יעַ זֶ֔רַע עֵ֣ץ פְּרִ֞י עֹ֤שֶׂה פְּרִי֙ לְמִינ֔וֹ אֲשֶׁ֥ר זַרְעוֹ־ב֖וֹ עַל־הָאָ֑רֶץ וַֽיְהִי־כֵֽן׃ ¹² וַתּוֹצֵ֨א הָאָ֜רֶץ דֶּ֠שֶׁא עֵ֣שֶׂב מַזְרִ֤יעַ זֶ֙רַע֙ לְמִינֵ֔הוּ וְעֵ֧ץ עֹֽשֶׂה־פְּרִ֛י אֲשֶׁ֥ר זַרְעוֹ־ב֖וֹ לְמִינֵ֑הוּ וַיַּ֥רְא אֱלֹהִ֖ים כִּי־טֽוֹב׃ ¹³ וַֽיְהִי־עֶ֥רֶב וַֽיְהִי־בֹ֖קֶר י֥וֹם שְׁלִישִֽׁי׃

⁹And Allah said, "Let the waters under the sky be gathered to one place and let dry ground appear." And it was so. ¹⁰Allah called the dry ground "land", and the gathered waters he called "sea". And Allah saw that it was good. ¹¹And Allah said, "Let the land produce vegetation, seed bearing plants and trees on the land that bear fruit with seed in it, according to their various kinds." And it was so. ¹²The land produced vegetation: plants bearing seed according to their kinds and trees bearing fruit with seeds in it according to their kinds. And Allah saw that it was good. ¹³And there was evening and there was morning, the third day.

Allah continues his work of dividing and separating what he has made.

Allah names his creation. On day one of creation, we read, "Allah called the light day, and the darkness He called night." He names the sky, the land and the sea. This shows Allah's rule and ownership over creation, just as today an inventor will give a name to his invention, or a human ruler who builds a new city will give it a name. The Qur'an also teaches Allah's sovereignty over His creation: "Know you not that to Allah belongs the dominion of the heavens and the earth" (al-Baqarah 2:107).

Then Allah creates life. He causes the earth to produce plants, trees and vegetation. Allah made these plants contain seeds to enable them to reproduce.

When you wander through forest and meadow, or when you enjoy the scent of wild roses or gaze at blossom in Spring-time, remember that Allah made this beautiful, vibrant, green world in which we live. To Him be thanks and praise.

Du'a: "Praise the LORD from the earth... you mountains and all hills, fruit trees and all cedars... Let them praise the Name of the LORD, for His Name alone is exalted; His splendour is above the earth and the heavens." (Zabur 148:7,9,13)

Day 5

Al-Taurat - Genesis 1:14-19

14 וַיֹּאמֶר אֱלֹהִים יְהִי מְאֹרֹת בִּרְקִיעַ הַשָּׁמַיִם
לְהַבְדִּיל בֵּין הַיֹּום וּבֵין הַלָּיְלָה וְהָיוּ לְאֹתֹת
וּלְמֹועֲדִים וּלְיָמִים וְשָׁנִים: 15 וְהָיוּ לִמְאֹורֹת
בִּרְקִיעַ הַשָּׁמַיִם לְהָאִיר עַל־הָאָרֶץ וַיְהִי־כֵן:
16 וַיַּעַשׂ אֱלֹהִים אֶת־שְׁנֵי הַמְּאֹרֹת הַגְּדֹלִים
אֶת־הַמָּאֹור הַגָּדֹל לְמֶמְשֶׁלֶת הַיֹּום וְאֶת־הַמָּאֹור
הַקָּטֹן לְמֶמְשֶׁלֶת הַלַּיְלָה וְאֵת הַכֹּוכָבִים:
17 וַיִּתֵּן אֹתָם אֱלֹהִים בִּרְקִיעַ הַשָּׁמָיִם לְהָאִיר
עַל־הָאָרֶץ: 18 וְלִמְשֹׁל בַּיֹּום וּבַלַּיְלָה וּלֲהַבְדִּיל
בֵּין הָאֹור וּבֵין הַחֹשֶׁךְ וַיַּרְא אֱלֹהִים כִּי־טֹוב:
19 וַיְהִי־עֶרֶב וַיְהִי־בֹקֶר יֹום רְבִיעִי:

14And Allah said, "Let there be lights in the expanse of the sky to separate the day from the night and let them be signs to mark seasons and days and years. 15And let there be lights in the expanse of the sky to shine upon the earth." And it was so. 16Allah made the two great lights; the greater light to rule over the day and the lesser light to rule over the night. And he made the stars. 17Allah placed them in the expanse of the sky to shine upon the earth, 18to rule the day and the night and to divide between the light and the darkness. And Allah saw that it was good. 19And there was evening and there was morning, the fourth day.

When Allah revealed al-Taurat through the Prophet Musa many people worshipped the sun, the moon and the stars. They believed that the stars controlled human destiny. Many people still believe these things today.

Here in al-Taurat, the sun, moon and stars are put in their proper place. Allah made them. They mark the passage of time, separate day from night and provide light on the earth. The sun and moon are simply called the greater and the lesser lights. That is because the names for sun and moon were also used to refer to the sun-god and the moon-god. But the sun and moon are not gods. They are simply part of Allah's great creation. "It is He (Allah) Who created the night and the day and the sun and the moon" (Qur'an, al-Anbiya 21:33).

The stars get only the briefest mention; "and he made the stars." The stars are amazing and beautiful, but they do not control our destiny. Our lives are in Allah's hands alone. We should not go to astrologers to find out our future. Instead we should commit our lives to Allah's care.

Du'a: *"You do we worship and Your aid we seek. Show us the straight way, The way of those on whom You have bestowed Your Grace, those whose (portion) is not wrath, and who go not astray."* (Qur'an, al-Fatihah 1:5-7)

Day 6

Al-Taurat - Genesis 1:20-23

²⁰ וַיֹּאמֶר אֱלֹהִים יִשְׁרְצוּ הַמַּיִם שֶׁרֶץ נֶפֶשׁ
חַיָּה וְעוֹף יְעוֹפֵף עַל־הָאָרֶץ עַל־פְּנֵי רְקִיעַ
הַשָּׁמָיִם: ²¹ וַיִּבְרָא אֱלֹהִים אֶת־הַתַּנִּינִם
הַגְּדֹלִים וְאֵת כָּל־נֶפֶשׁ הַחַיָּה। הָרֹמֶשֶׂת
אֲשֶׁר שָׁרְצוּ הַמַּיִם לְמִינֵהֶם וְאֵת כָּל־עוֹף
כָּנָף לְמִינֵהוּ וַיַּרְא אֱלֹהִים כִּי־טוֹב:
²² וַיְבָרֶךְ אֹתָם אֱלֹהִים לֵאמֹר פְּרוּ וּרְבוּ
וּמִלְאוּ אֶת־הַמַּיִם בַּיַּמִּים וְהָעוֹף יִרֶב
בָּאָרֶץ: ²³ וַיְהִי־עֶרֶב וַיְהִי־בֹקֶר יוֹם חֲמִישִׁי:

²⁰And Allah said, "Let the water teem with living creatures and let birds fly over the earth, across the expanse of the sky." ²¹And Allah created the great sea creatures and all the moving living creatures which teem in the waters according to their kinds and all winged birds according to their kinds. And Allah saw that it was good. ²²And Allah blessed them saying, "Be fruitful and increase in number and fill the waters of the seas, and let the birds increase on the earth." ²³And there was evening and there was morning, the fifth day.

There is another step forward in the process of creation: Allah creates animals that live and move in the sea and in the sky.

These verses present a picture of the seas and sky abounding and pulsating with life. There is a vast and varied number of species. One biologist estimates that there may be around 30 million different species of animal and plant, but admits that nobody knows. However, Allah knows because He created each one. How great, how vast is Allah's wisdom, knowledge and power!

Allah also blesses them. He grants wholeness and life to the full. He gives the ability to be fruitful and increase in number. In this way, new life is reproduced so that they will fill the seas and the air.

In this way Allah's work of creation continues throughout history, as each new generation is Allah's creation.

Du'a: "How many are your works O LORD! In wisdom you made them all; the earth is full of your creatures. There is the sea, vast and spacious, teeming with creatures beyond number - living things both large and small." (Zabur 104:24-25)

Day 7

Al-Taurat - Genesis 1:24-25

²⁴ וַיֹּאמֶר אֱלֹהִים תּוֹצֵא הָאָרֶץ נֶפֶשׁ חַיָּה
לְמִינָהּ בְּהֵמָה וָרֶמֶשׂ וְחַיְתוֹ־אֶרֶץ לְמִינָהּ
וַיְהִי־כֵן: ²⁵ וַיַּעַשׂ אֱלֹהִים אֶת־חַיַּת הָאָרֶץ
לְמִינָהּ וְאֶת־הַבְּהֵמָה לְמִינָהּ וְאֵת כָּל־
רֶמֶשׂ הָאֲדָמָה לְמִינֵהוּ וַיַּרְא אֱלֹהִים כִּי־
טוֹב:

²⁴And Allah said, "Let the earth produce living creatures according to their kinds, livestock, creatures that move along the ground and wild animals according to their kinds." And it was so. ²⁵And Allah made the wild animals according to their kinds and the livestock according to their kinds, and all the creatures that move along the ground according to their kinds. And Allah saw that it was good.

Allah now makes creatures of the land, including mammals. Among these too, there is a vast variety of species or kinds. Some of the peoples who lived at the time al-Taurat was revealed through Prophet Musa, worshipped gods in the form of animals. The ancient Egyptians practised this kind of religion. Here al-Taurat makes it clear that these animals are not gods to be worshipped. Instead, they are creatures made by the One True Allah. The vast variety, beauty and complexity of these creatures speak to us of Allah's glory and praise.

We will see from tomorrow's reading that the land animals are made on the same day as human beings. Land animals were also produced from the earth, as was the first man. Animals and humans have this in common: they are both creatures, made by the Creator. Biologically, animals, especially mammals, have many things in common with humans. However, what makes humans different from animals is far more important than the things that are similar. We will begin to look at some of these things in tomorrow's reading.

Du'a: "Praise the LORD. Praise Allah in His sanctuary; praise Him in His mighty heavens. Praise Him for His acts of power; praise Him for His surpassing greatness... Let everything that has breath praise the LORD." (Zabur 150:1,2,6)

Day 8

Al-Taurat - Genesis 1:26-28

²⁶ וַיֹּאמֶר אֱלֹהִים נַעֲשֶׂה אָדָם בְּצַלְמֵנוּ
כִּדְמוּתֵנוּ וְיִרְדּוּ בִדְגַת הַיָּם וּבְעוֹף הַשָּׁמַיִם
וּבַבְּהֵמָה וּבְכָל־הָאָרֶץ וּבְכָל־הָרֶמֶשׂ הָרֹמֵשׂ
עַל־הָאָרֶץ: ²⁷ וַיִּבְרָא אֱלֹהִים אֶת־הָאָדָם
בְּצַלְמוֹ בְּצֶלֶם אֱלֹהִים בָּרָא אֹתוֹ זָכָר
וּנְקֵבָה בָּרָא אֹתָם: ²⁸ וַיְבָרֶךְ אֹתָם אֱלֹהִים
וַיֹּאמֶר לָהֶם אֱלֹהִים פְּרוּ וּרְבוּ וּמִלְאוּ אֶת־
הָאָרֶץ וְכִבְשֻׁהָ וּרְדוּ בִדְגַת הַיָּם וּבְעוֹף
הַשָּׁמַיִם וּבְכָל־חַיָּה הָרֹמֶשֶׂת עַל־הָאָרֶץ:

²⁶And Allah said, "Let us make human beings in our image, in our likeness, and let them rule over the fish of the sea and the birds of the air and over the livestock and over all the earth and over all the creatures that move on the earth." ²⁷So Allah created human beings in his own image, in the image of Allah he created them, male and female he created them. ²⁸And Allah blessed them and Allah said to them, "Be fruitful and increase in number, fill the earth and subdue it. Rule over the fish of the sea and the birds of the air and over all living creatures that move on the earth."

"Who am I?" This is one of the most basic and important questions a person can ask. If I don't understand myself, how can I understand anything? Many people are lost today because they don't know who they are.

Identity is important in our world today. There are many factors that make up our identity. I belong to a family, a clan or *biradari*, a nation, a religious community, a culture. I speak a particular language, I have certain abilities and interests, and so on. However, at root, I am a human being – that is the most basic thing about me. But what does it mean to be human?

Al-Taurat provides an answer to this question of our identity as humans. Al-Taurat tells me who I am.

Du'a: *"When I consider your heavens, the work of Your fingers, the moon and the stars, which You have set in place, what is a human being that You are mindful of him, the son of man that You care for him? You have made him a little lower than the heavenly beings and crowned him with glory and honour. You made them rulers over the works of Your hands; and put everything under their feet."* (Zabur 8:3-6)

Day 9

Read Again
Al-Taurat - Genesis 1:26-28

²⁶ וַיֹּ֣אמֶר אֱלֹהִ֗ים נַֽעֲשֶׂ֥ה אָדָ֛ם בְּצַלְמֵ֖נוּ
כִּדְמוּתֵ֑נוּ וְיִרְדּוּ֩ בִדְגַ֨ת הַיָּ֜ם וּבְע֣וֹף הַשָּׁמַ֗יִם
וּבַבְּהֵמָה֙ וּבְכָל־הָאָ֔רֶץ וּבְכָל־הָרֶ֖מֶשׂ הָֽרֹמֵ֥שׂ
עַל־הָאָֽרֶץ: ²⁷ וַיִּבְרָ֨א אֱלֹהִ֤ים׀ אֶת־הָֽאָדָם֙
בְּצַלְמ֔וֹ בְּצֶ֥לֶם אֱלֹהִ֖ים בָּרָ֣א אֹת֑וֹ זָכָ֥ר
וּנְקֵבָ֖ה בָּרָ֥א אֹתָֽם: ²⁸ וַיְבָ֣רֶךְ אֹתָם֮ אֱלֹהִים֒
וַיֹּ֨אמֶר לָהֶ֜ם אֱלֹהִ֗ים פְּר֥וּ וּרְב֛וּ וּמִלְא֥וּ אֶת־
הָאָ֖רֶץ וְכִבְשֻׁ֑הָ וּרְד֞וּ בִּדְגַ֤ת הַיָּם֙ וּבְע֣וֹף
הַשָּׁמַ֔יִם וּבְכָל־חַיָּ֖ה הָֽרֹמֶ֥שֶׂת עַל־הָאָֽרֶץ:

²⁶And Allah said, "Let us make human beings
in our image, in our likeness, and let them rule
over the fish of the sea and the birds of the air
and over the livestock and over all the earth
and over all the creatures that move on the
earth." ²⁷So Allah created human beings in his
own image, in the image of Allah he created
them, male and female he created them. ²⁸And
Allah blessed them and Allah said to them,
"Be fruitful and increase in number, fill the
earth and subdue it. Rule over the fish of the
sea and the birds of the air and over all living
creatures that move on the earth."

Al-Taurat tells us that we are creatures, made by Allah. We have this in common with the rest of creation. But human beings are also distinct from other creatures. In this account of creation, there are characteristics that make humans unique.

The word translated "human beings" is actually *adam* in the original Hebrew text. This is the name of the first man - Adam. In Hebrew, the word can also refer to an individual human being or to humanity as a race.

Allah uses a unique form of words in the creation of humans. He does not use these words when creating anything else. Allah says, "Let Us make human beings in Our image, in Our likeness..." A little further on it says, "Allah created human beings in His own image, in the image of Allah He created them..."

The words "image of Allah" may be misunderstood as they may cause some people to think of idols and visual representations of Allah. In fact, these words are the very opposite of that. Here it is Allah who makes humans and places his image and likeness in them. In idol worship, it is the other way round – humans make images, and then claim they represent Allah. This practice is forbidden in al-Taurat in the second commandment of the Sharia given to Prophet Musa:

"You shall not make for yourselves an idol in the form of anything in heaven above or on the earth beneath or in the waters below. You shall not bow down to them or worship them..." (Al-Taurat - Exodus 20:4-5).

Du'a: "I praise You because I am fearfully and wonderfully made." (Zabur 139:14)

Day 10

Read Again
Al-Taurat - Genesis 1:26-28

²⁶ וַיֹּאמֶר אֱלֹהִים נַעֲשֶׂה אָדָם בְּצַלְמֵנוּ
כִּדְמוּתֵנוּ וְיִרְדּוּ בִדְגַת הַיָּם וּבְעוֹף הַשָּׁמַיִם
וּבַבְּהֵמָה וּבְכָל־הָאָרֶץ וּבְכָל־הָרֶמֶשׂ הָרֹמֵשׂ
עַל־הָאָרֶץ: ²⁷ וַיִּבְרָא אֱלֹהִים אֶת־הָאָדָם
בְּצַלְמוֹ בְּצֶלֶם אֱלֹהִים בָּרָא אֹתוֹ זָכָר
וּנְקֵבָה בָּרָא אֹתָם: ²⁸ וַיְבָרֶךְ אֹתָם אֱלֹהִים
וַיֹּאמֶר לָהֶם אֱלֹהִים פְּרוּ וּרְבוּ וּמִלְאוּ אֶת־
הָאָרֶץ וְכִבְשֻׁהָ וּרְדוּ בִדְגַת הַיָּם וּבְעוֹף
הַשָּׁמַיִם וּבְכָל־חַיָּה הָרֹמֶשֶׂת עַל־הָאָרֶץ:

²⁶And Allah said, "Let us make human beings in our image, in our likeness, and let them rule over the fish of the sea and the birds of the air and over the livestock and over all the earth and over all the creatures that move on the earth." ²⁷So Allah created human beings in his own image, in the image of Allah he created them, male and female he created them. ²⁸And Allah blessed them and Allah said to them, "Be fruitful and increase in number, fill the earth and subdue it. Rule over the fish of the sea and the birds of the air and over all living creatures that move on the earth."

What does it mean to be made in the image and likeness of Allah? Probably it includes everything in humans that is distinct from other creatures and that corresponds in some way to what Allah is like.

In v.26 and v.28 Allah gives humans the task of ruling over the rest of creation. Of course, Allah is still the supreme Ruler over His creation, but he delegates rule to humans. Adam is a *khalifah* (Qur'an, al-Baqarah 2:30). Our task of ruling over and subduing the earth is expressed in many different activities such as farming, building, arts, science, technology, education and study. We are also to "be fruitful and increase in number." This means we are to have children. All these are good and halaal activities because they are part of the purpose for which Allah made us.

In v.28 we read, "Allah said to them…" Already we have seen that Allah is a speaking Being. He speaks things into existence. But here, for the first time, Allah speaks directly *to* some part of his creation. He speaks *to* these humans. This tells us much about ourselves. Unlike animals, humans have rational minds. Humans were made to hear Allah speak and understand what He says. And humans were given the ability to respond by speaking back.

Allah's speaking to these first humans tells us that we alone as humans are made for relationship with Allah. He has made us with the potential to hear His voice, to receive His revelation. And Allah has made us with the ability to respond back in prayer and worship. In other words, humans are spiritual beings. We are religious beings with an awareness of Allah.

Du'a: Help me, Allah, to hear Your word and obey, to love You and live for Your praise.

Day 11

Read Again
Al-Taurat - Genesis 1:26-28

²⁶ וַיֹּ֣אמֶר אֱלֹהִ֔ים נַֽעֲשֶׂ֥ה אָדָ֛ם בְּצַלְמֵ֖נוּ
כִּדְמוּתֵ֑נוּ וְיִרְדּוּ֩ בִדְגַ֨ת הַיָּ֜ם וּבְע֣וֹף הַשָּׁמַ֗יִם
וּבַבְּהֵמָה֙ וּבְכָל־הָאָ֔רֶץ וּבְכָל־הָרֶ֖מֶשׂ הָֽרֹמֵ֥שׂ
עַל־הָאָֽרֶץ: ²⁷ וַיִּבְרָ֨א אֱלֹהִ֤ים ׀ אֶת־הָֽאָדָם֙
בְּצַלְמ֔וֹ בְּצֶ֥לֶם אֱלֹהִ֖ים בָּרָ֣א אֹת֑וֹ זָכָ֥ר
וּנְקֵבָ֖ה בָּרָ֥א אֹתָֽם: ²⁸ וַיְבָ֣רֶךְ אֹתָם֮ אֱלֹהִים֒
וַיֹּ֨אמֶר לָהֶ֜ם אֱלֹהִ֗ים פְּר֥וּ וּרְב֛וּ וּמִלְא֥וּ אֶת־
הָאָ֖רֶץ וְכִבְשֻׁ֑הָ וּרְד֞וּ בִּדְגַ֤ת הַיָּם֙ וּבְע֣וֹף
הַשָּׁמַ֔יִם וּבְכָל־חַיָּ֖ה הָֽרֹמֶ֥שֶׂת עַל־הָאָֽרֶץ:

²⁶And Allah said, "Let us make human beings
in our image, in our likeness, and let them rule
over the fish of the sea and the birds of the air
and over the livestock and over all the earth
and over all the creatures that move on the
earth." ²⁷So Allah created human beings in his
own image, in the image of Allah he created
them, male and female he created them. ²⁸And
Allah blessed them and Allah said to them,
"Be fruitful and increase in number, fill the
earth and subdue it. Rule over the fish of the
sea and the birds of the air and over all living
creatures that move on the earth."

Humans are made in the image and likeness of Allah. Thus they are unique and special, the crowning glory of Allah's creation.

We were also made to speak and relate to other humans. In v.27 we read, "...male and female He created them." This is the most basic distinction within the human race. Both male and female humans are made in Allah's image and likeness. This means that, although men and women are different in many ways, they are equal in value and significance.

So we should not think of women as being inferior to men. We should rejoice and give thanks to Allah as much for the birth of a girl as for a boy. We should respect and love daughters as much as sons.

Al-Taurat's teaching about who we are as human beings should affect the way we relate to ourselves and to other people. You have great value, your life is sacred, because you are made in Allah's image and likeness. We should show great respect and honour for every human being, because every one is made in Allah's image and likeness. This is why murder is such a terrible sin. We should show respect and honour even to those who are poor, weak and sick and those who have low status in the eyes of the world. We should show such respect and honour to all people, whatever their race, culture or religion. This is why Allah commands us to "love your neighbour as yourself" (al-Taurat: Leviticus 19:18).

Du'a: Allah, help me to see people as You see them. Help me to treat every human life as precious. Help me to love my neighbour as myself.

Day 12

Al-Taurat - Genesis 1:29-30

²⁹ וַיֹּאמֶר אֱלֹהִים הִנֵּה נָתַתִּי לָכֶם אֶת־
כָּל־עֵשֶׂב ׀ זֹרֵעַ זֶרַע אֲשֶׁר עַל־פְּנֵי כָל־
הָאָרֶץ וְאֶת־כָּל־הָעֵץ אֲשֶׁר־בּוֹ פְרִי־עֵץ
זֹרֵעַ זָרַע לָכֶם יִהְיֶה לְאָכְלָה: ³⁰ וּלְכָל־
חַיַּת הָאָרֶץ וּלְכָל־עוֹף הַשָּׁמַיִם וּלְכֹל ׀
רוֹמֵשׂ עַל־הָאָרֶץ אֲשֶׁר־בּוֹ נֶפֶשׁ חַיָּה
אֶת־כָּל־יֶרֶק עֵשֶׂב לְאָכְלָה וַיְהִי־כֵן:

²⁹And Allah said, "Look, I give you every seed-bearing plant on the face of the whole earth and every tree that has fruit with seed in it. They will be yours for food. ³⁰And to every living creature of the earth and every bird of the air and everything that moves on the ground that has the breath of life in it – I give every green plant for food. And it was so.

Allah has made human beings and a world full of many different creatures. Now Allah, in His goodness provides food for his creatures. He has created vegetables and fruit to be nourishing, tasty and life-giving. At this time meat was not eaten. That was part of the harmony of the original creation. Only later in the time of Prophet Nuh, Allah allows meat to be eaten.

Many pagan people take offerings of food to their gods. People think they are providing their gods with food. But al-Taurat shows that such practises are completely the wrong way round. We don't provide food for Allah; He provides food for us – and for all the creatures He has made. He is *al-Razzaq*, the Provider. In the same way the Qur'an teaches: "It is Allah Who… has provided for you sustenance of things pure and good" (al-Mumin 40:64).

Today also Allah is the One who supplies our daily food. Many people in the world today go hungry, but this is not because Allah fails to provide enough food for everybody. Hunger is caused by human greed. We should give thanks to Allah for His kindness and goodness towards us. We should share the good things we have received with those who are in need. We should work for justice for the world's poor.

Du'a: *Allah, I thank You that You sustain our lives every day and You provide for all our needs. Grant us food this day. May we be willing to share with those who are in need. Help us to work for a more just and fair world.*

Day 13

Al-Taurat - Genesis 1:31

³¹ וַיַּרְא אֱלֹהִים אֶת־כָּל־אֲשֶׁר
עָשָׂה וְהִנֵּה־טוֹב מְאֹד וַיְהִי־
עֶרֶב וַיְהִי־בֹקֶר יוֹם הַשִּׁשִּׁי׃

³¹And Allah saw everything that he had made, that it was very good. And there was evening and there was morning, the sixth day.

Allah finishes his work of creation. He then sees his work and takes pleasure in it, like an artist who stands back and surveys his finished work with satisfaction.

Allah declares the creation "very good". The word "good" in the Hebrew language of the original text can mean pleasant, beautiful, delightful, joyful, correct and righteous.

Everything was very good. There was nothing that was bad or wrong or evil in the whole of creation. Allah's work is perfect.

But now we cannot say that *everything* is very good. It is true that by Allah's mercy there is still much that is good, beautiful and enjoyable. But everything is no longer very good. We all recognise that we don't live in that kind of a world any more. Now we see things that are bad, ugly and evil. We experience suffering, misery, disease and death.

We must realise that the way the world is now is not the way Allah created it. Allah is good, and all His work is good. Allah is not the author of evil. In fact goodness is ultimately based on the character of Allah Himself. Evil, or sin is all that goes against Allah and His will.

Later on we will look at the origin of evil in the world. But Allah Himself is *al-Quddus*, the Holy One (see Qur'an, al-Hashr 59:23). This means Allah is completely separate from all that is evil.

Du'a: *"You are good, and what You do is good; teach me Your decrees."* (Zabur 119:68)

Day 14

Al-Taurat - Genesis 2:1-3

1 וַיְכֻלּ֛וּ הַשָּׁמַ֥יִם וְהָאָ֖רֶץ וְכָל־צְבָאָֽם׃

2 וַיְכַ֤ל אֱלֹהִים֙ בַּיּ֣וֹם הַשְּׁבִיעִ֔י
מְלַאכְתּ֖וֹ אֲשֶׁ֣ר עָשָׂ֑ה וַיִּשְׁבֹּת֙ בַּיּ֣וֹם
הַשְּׁבִיעִ֔י מִכָּל־מְלַאכְתּ֖וֹ אֲשֶׁ֥ר עָשָֽׂה׃

3 וַיְבָ֤רֶךְ אֱלֹהִים֙ אֶת־י֣וֹם הַשְּׁבִיעִ֔י
וַיְקַדֵּ֖שׁ אֹת֑וֹ כִּ֣י ב֤וֹ שָׁבַת֙ מִכָּל־
מְלַאכְתּ֔וֹ אֲשֶׁר־בָּרָ֥א אֱלֹהִ֖ים לַעֲשֽׂוֹת׃

¹Thus the heavens and the earth were completed and all their vast array. ²And by the seventh day Allah completed the work He had done, and He rested on the seventh day from all the work that He had done. ³And Allah blessed the seventh day and made it holy, because on it He rested from all the work of creating that He had done.

Allah finishes His work of creating the heavens and the earth and the "vast array" they contain.

When we read that Allah rested, it does not mean that Allah was tired and needed a rest. Instead it means that Allah stopped His work because He had finished it.

> The LORD is the everlasting Allah, the creator of the ends of the earth, He will not grow tired or weary and His understanding no-one can fathom (Isaiah 40:28).

Of course, there is a sense in which Allah's work of creation continues. All the time He sustains and rules over His creation. Allah continuously governs the processes of re-creation, birth, growth and development.

Allah also blessed the seventh day and made it holy. This is the basis for the fourth command in the Sharia given to Prophet Musa: "Remember the Sabbath day by keeping it holy" (Al-Taurat – Exodus 20:8). The children of Israel were to rest on the seventh (Sabbath) day of the week. It was to be a day specially set aside for remembering Allah.

It is still good to keep one day in seven for rest and worship. Allah gives a blessing to those who do this.

Du'a: "It is good to praise the LORD... for You make me glad by Your deeds LORD; I sing for joy at what Your hands have done. How great are Your works, LORD, how profound your thoughts!" (Zabur 92:1, 4-5)

Day 15

Al-Taurat - Genesis 2:4-7

⁴ אֵ֣לֶּה תוֹלְד֧וֹת הַשָּׁמַ֛יִם וְהָאָ֖רֶץ בְּהִבָּֽרְאָ֑ם בְּי֗וֹם עֲשׂ֛וֹת יְהוָ֥ה אֱלֹהִ֖ים אֶ֥רֶץ וְשָׁמָֽיִם׃ ⁵ וְכֹ֣ל ׀ שִׂ֣יחַ הַשָּׂדֶ֗ה טֶ֚רֶם יִֽהְיֶ֣ה בָאָ֔רֶץ וְכָל־עֵ֥שֶׂב הַשָּׂדֶ֖ה טֶ֣רֶם יִצְמָ֑ח כִּי֩ לֹ֨א הִמְטִ֜יר יְהוָ֤ה אֱלֹהִים֙ עַל־הָאָ֔רֶץ וְאָדָ֣ם אַ֔יִן לַֽעֲבֹ֖ד אֶת־ הָֽאֲדָמָֽה׃ ⁶ וְאֵ֖ד יַֽעֲלֶ֣ה מִן־הָאָ֑רֶץ וְהִשְׁקָ֖ה אֶֽת־ כָּל־פְּנֵֽי־הָֽאֲדָמָֽה׃ ⁷ וַיִּיצֶר֩ יְהוָ֨ה אֱלֹהִ֜ים אֶת־הָֽאָדָ֗ם עָפָר֙ מִן־הָ֣אֲדָמָ֔ה וַיִּפַּ֥ח בְּאַפָּ֖יו נִשְׁמַ֣ת חַיִּ֑ים וַֽיְהִ֥י הָֽאָדָ֖ם לְנֶ֥פֶשׁ חַיָּֽה׃

⁴These are the accounts of the heavens and the earth when they were created, in the day the LORD Allah made the earth and the heavens. ⁵Now no shrub of the field had yet grown on the earth, and no plant of the field had yet sprung up, because the LORD Allah had not made it rain on the earth, and there was no man to work the ground. ⁶But streams came up from the earth and watered all the surface of the ground. ⁷And the LORD Allah formed a man from the dust of the ground, and breathed into his nostrils the breath of life, and the man became a living creature.

We find a new title for Allah in these verses. He is "the LORD Allah". "LORD," written in capital letters, is how most English versions translate the Hebrew name for Allah which is "Yahweh".

In v.7 we read that "the LORD Allah formed a man from the dust of the ground". This is like the action of a potter forming and shaping items out of clay. The material Allah uses is the dust of the ground (see Qur'an, al-Imran 3:59).

Then Allah "breathed into his nostrils the breath of life." The Qur'an in a similar way says, "I (Allah) have fashioned him (in due proportion) and breathed into him of My spirit" (al-Hijr 15:29). This is only said of the creation of humans and points to humans being special.

These verses tell us very clearly that humans are Allah's creatures. Our lives are not our own; they belong to Allah. Even the breath you breathe at this second is a gift from the Almighty. One day we will each have to give an account to Allah for what we have done with the lives He has given us. "We will all give an account of ourselves to Allah" (Injil, Romans 14:12).

Du'a: Allah, You give to me my life, my breath and everything I have. May I live as one who will give an account for my life. May my life be lived for Your glory.

Day 16

Al-Taurat - Genesis 2:8-9

⁸ וַיִּטַּע יְהוָה אֱלֹהִים גַּן־בְּעֵדֶן מִקֶּדֶם
וַיָּשֶׂם שָׁם אֶת־הָאָדָם אֲשֶׁר יָצָר:
⁹ וַיַּצְמַח יְהוָה אֱלֹהִים מִן־הָאֲדָמָה
כָּל־עֵץ נֶחְמָד לְמַרְאֶה וְטוֹב לְמַאֲכָל
וְעֵץ הַחַיִּים בְּתוֹךְ הַגָּן וְעֵץ הַדַּעַת
טוֹב וָרָע:

⁸Now the LORD Allah planted a garden in Eden in the east. There he put the man he had formed. ⁹The LORD Allah made all kinds of trees grow out of the ground – trees that were pleasing to the eye and good for food. The tree of life was in the middle of the garden and the tree of the knowledge of good and evil.

Eden means "delight." There, the LORD Allah planted a garden (translated paradise in many early translations of al-Taurat). Allah put the man there. This was to be his home and environment.

Allah caused all kinds of trees to grow. Allah creates amazing variety and diversity. The trees were "pleasing to the eye." Allah creates beauty and loves beauty. We too should value beauty.

There were also trees that were good for food. The word "good" here suggests more than just sufficient to keep the man alive. It suggests food that is delicious, healthy and abundant.

In the middle of the garden was the tree of life. The fruit of this tree was a sign or symbol for Adam that he depended on Allah for life. This life was eternal. Allah originally made humans to live for ever. Every time Adam ate of the fruit of this tree, he would be reminded that life is Allah's gift.

There was also the tree of the knowledge of good and evil. We will return to this later.

Du'a: Allah, thank You that You create beauty and that even now we can enjoy so much that is beautiful in Your world.

Day 17

Al-Taurat - Genesis 2:10-15

10 וְנָהָר֙ יֹצֵ֣א מֵעֵ֔דֶן לְהַשְׁק֖וֹת אֶת־הַגָּ֑ן וּמִשָּׁם֙ יִפָּרֵ֔ד וְהָיָ֖ה לְאַרְבָּעָ֥ה רָאשִֽׁים׃ 11 שֵׁ֥ם הָֽאֶחָ֖ד פִּישׁ֑וֹן ה֣וּא הַסֹּבֵ֗ב אֵ֚ת כָּל־אֶ֣רֶץ הַֽחֲוִילָ֔ה אֲשֶׁר־שָׁ֖ם הַזָּהָֽב׃ 12 וּֽזֲהַ֛ב הָאָ֥רֶץ הַהִ֖וא ט֑וֹב שָׁ֥ם הַבְּדֹ֖לַח וְאֶ֥בֶן הַשֹּֽׁהַם׃ 13 וְשֵֽׁם־הַנָּהָ֖ר הַשֵּׁנִ֣י גִּיח֑וֹן ה֣וּא הַסּוֹבֵ֔ב אֵ֖ת כָּל־אֶ֥רֶץ כּֽוּשׁ׃ 14 וְשֵׁ֨ם הַנָּהָ֤ר הַשְּׁלִישִׁי֙ חִדֶּ֔קֶל ה֥וּא הַֽהֹלֵ֖ךְ קִדְמַ֣ת אַשּׁ֑וּר וְהַנָּהָ֥ר הָֽרְבִיעִ֖י ה֥וּא פְרָֽת׃ 15 וַיִּקַּ֛ח יְהוָ֥ה אֱלֹהִ֖ים אֶת־הָֽאָדָ֑ם וַיַּנִּחֵ֣הוּ בְגַן־עֵ֔דֶן לְעָבְדָ֖הּ וּלְשָׁמְרָֽהּ׃

¹⁰A river watering the garden was flowing from Eden. From there it divided into four head waters. ¹¹The name of the first is the Pishon, it winds through the entire land of Havilah, where there is gold. ¹²The gold of that land is good. Aromatic resin and onyx are also there. ¹³The name of the second river is the Gihon. It winds through the entire land of Cush. ¹⁴The name of the third river is the Tigris. It flows along the east side of Ashur. And the fourth river is the Euphrates. ¹⁵The LORD Allah took the man and put him in the garden of Eden to work it and take care of it.

Water is essential for life. This river provided for the abundant variety of life in the garden.

Allah places the man in the Garden of Eden. He is given a task to do - working and taking care of the garden. Man was made to work, and work was a blessing. Unemployment is not good for people. Every society should aim for full employment.

Working and taking care of the garden would involve physical work. Some societies despise physical, manual labour as having low status. But al-Taurat gives it dignity and honour.

The man must also take care of the garden. He is responsible for looking after his environment. We as humans today still have this responsibility. That means that we must try to conserve the environment and reduce and stop pollution. We should avoid waste. We must develop our world in a way that protects and sustains the environment. Allah demands this of us.

"Green" issues are a matter of great concern in our world today. It is amazing that al-Taurat is so ancient, and yet speaks to the issues of the twenty-first Century.

Du'a: Allah, help us to take care of Your creation. Help us to adopt life-styles that do not waste resources and pollute the environment. Help us to develop our surroundings in a way that sustains the creation.

$\mathcal{D}$ay 18

Al-Taurat - Genesis 2:16-17

¹⁶ וַיְצַו֙ יְהוָ֣ה אֱלֹהִ֔ים עַל־הָֽאָדָ֖ם
לֵאמֹ֑ר מִכֹּ֥ל עֵֽץ־הַגָּ֖ן אָכֹ֥ל תֹּאכֵֽל:
¹⁷ וּמֵעֵ֗ץ הַדַּ֨עַת֙ ט֣וֹב וָרָ֔ע לֹ֥א
תֹאכַ֖ל מִמֶּ֑נּוּ כִּ֗י בְּי֛וֹם אֲכָלְךָ֥
מִמֶּ֖נּוּ מ֥וֹת תָּמֽוּת:

¹⁶And the LORD Allah
commanded the man: "You may
eat from every tree in the garden.
¹⁷But you must not eat from the tree
of the knowledge of good and evil,
for when you eat from it you will
certainly die."

The LORD Allah was very generous to the man. He allowed the man to eat from every tree in the garden, except one. Adam had an amazing variety of wonderful food to choose from. Likewise in the Qur'an, Allah says, "O Adam! Dwell you and your wife in the garden and eat of the bountiful things in it as (when and where) you will" (al-Baqarah 2:35).

There was one tree that Allah commanded Adam not to eat from – the tree of the knowledge of good and evil. The fruit of this tree was a sign or symbol for Adam. It reminded him that Allah is the One who decides what is good, and what is evil. This tree represented Allah's moral authority.

If Adam were to eat from this tree, he would disobey Allah's command. That would mean that Adam was rejecting Allah's authority. It would mean that Adam was appointing himself as the one who decided what was good and what was evil for him. It would mean Adam was declaring his independence from Allah. This is what sin is.

Allah warns Adam. There is a punishment for sin, and it is death.

Adam, and later Hawwa, were created perfect. They were part of Allah's original creation which Allah said was "very good" (see 1:31, Day 13). But Allah created humans with a free will – to choose obedience to Allah, or disobedience.

Du'a: "Keep your servant from wilful sins; may they not rule over me." (Zabur 19:13)

40

Day 19

Al-Taurat - Genesis 2:18-20

¹⁸ וַיֹּ֙אמֶר֙ יְהוָ֣ה אֱלֹהִ֔ים לֹא־ט֛וֹב הֱי֥וֹת
הָֽאָדָ֖ם לְבַדּ֑וֹ אֶֽעֱשֶׂה־לּ֥וֹ עֵ֖זֶר כְּנֶגְדּֽוֹ׃ ¹⁹ וַיִּצֶר֩
יְהוָ֨ה אֱלֹהִ֜ים מִן־הָֽאֲדָמָ֗ה כָּל־חַיַּ֤ת הַשָּׂדֶה֙
וְאֵת֙ כָּל־ע֣וֹף הַשָּׁמַ֔יִם וַיָּבֵא֙ אֶל־הָ֣אָדָ֔ם
לִרְא֖וֹת מַה־יִּקְרָא־ל֑וֹ וְכֹל֩ אֲשֶׁ֨ר יִקְרָא־
ל֧וֹ הָֽאָדָ֛ם נֶ֥פֶשׁ חַיָּ֖ה ה֥וּא שְׁמֽוֹ׃ ²⁰ וַיִּקְרָ֨א
הָֽאָדָ֜ם שֵׁמ֗וֹת לְכָל־הַבְּהֵמָה֙ וּלְע֣וֹף
הַשָּׁמַ֔יִם וּלְכֹ֖ל חַיַּ֣ת הַשָּׂדֶ֑ה

¹⁸The LORD Allah said, "It is not good for the man to be alone. I will make a helper suitable for him." ¹⁹The LORD Allah had formed from the ground every wild animal and every bird of the air, and he brought them to the man to see what he would name them. And everything the man named a living creature – that was its name. ²⁰So the man gave names to all the livestock and to the birds of the air and to all the wild animals.

41

In chapter one, when Allah is creating the universe, five times we read, "Allah saw that it was good." But here is one thing that is not good – that the man is alone. Amazingly Adam is at this time a perfect human being – he has a perfect relationship with Allah. Yet still he is "alone" and Allah says that is "not good." Humans are social beings, they need the company of others. That is the way Allah has made us. Allah knows Adam's needs and cares for him.

Allah brings the animals to Adam to name them. In chapter one Allah names different parts of his creation. This expresses Allah's rule. Allah made humans to rule over the rest of creation (1:26-28). He delegated rule to humans. Adam is a *khalifah* (Qur'an, al-Baqarah 2:30). One way in which this is expressed is by Adam naming the animals.

Human scientific activity has its origins here. A large part of science is to study some part of creation and then name or classify it. That is what Adam is doing here. There is no real conflict between science and religion. Science is only possible because Allah has made an orderly universe and has made human beings with the ability to observe, classify and rule over the rest of creation.

Du'a: Allah, Thank You that you know our needs and care for us. Thank You for family, friends, community and society.

Day 20

Al-Taurat - Genesis 2:20-25

וּלְאָדָ֕ם לֹֽא־מָצָ֥א עֵ֖זֶר כְּנֶגְדּֽוֹ׃ ²¹ וַיַּפֵּל֩ יְהֹוָ֨ה אֱלֹהִ֧ים ׀
תַּרְדֵּמָ֛ה עַל־הָֽאָדָ֖ם וַיִּישָׁ֑ן וַיִּקַּ֗ח אַחַת֙ מִצַּלְעֹתָ֔יו
וַיִּסְגֹּ֥ר בָּשָׂ֖ר תַּחְתֶּֽנָּה׃ ²² וַיִּ֩בֶן֩ יְהֹוָ֨ה אֱלֹהִ֧ים ׀ אֶֽת־
הַצֵּלָ֛ע אֲשֶׁר־לָקַ֥ח מִן־הָֽאָדָ֖ם לְאִשָּׁ֑ה וַיְבִאֶ֖הָ אֶל־
הָֽאָדָֽם׃ ²³ וַיֹּ֮אמֶר֮ הָֽאָדָם֒ זֹ֣את הַפַּ֗עַם עֶ֚צֶם מֵֽעֲצָמַ֔י
וּבָשָׂ֖ר מִבְּשָׂרִ֑י לְזֹאת֙ יִקָּרֵ֣א אִשָּׁ֔ה כִּ֥י מֵאִ֖ישׁ
לֻֽקְחָה־זֹּֽאת׃ ²⁴ עַל־כֵּן֙ יַֽעֲזׇב־אִ֔ישׁ אֶת־אָבִ֖יו וְאֶת־אִמּ֑וֹ
וְדָבַ֣ק בְּאִשְׁתּ֔וֹ וְהָי֖וּ לְבָשָׂ֥ר אֶחָֽד׃ ²⁵ וַיִּֽהְיוּ֙ שְׁנֵיהֶ֣ם
עֲרוּמִּ֔ים הָֽאָדָ֖ם וְאִשְׁתּ֑וֹ וְלֹ֖א יִתְבֹּשָֽׁשׁוּ׃

But for Adam no suitable helper was found.
²¹So the LORD Allah caused the man to fall
into a deep sleep. While he slept, the LORD
Allah took one of his ribs and closed round it with
flesh. ²²And the LORD Allah built the rib he had
taken from the man into a woman and He brought
her to the man. ²³The man said, "At last, this is
bone of my bone and flesh of my flesh. She will be
called 'woman' because she was taken from man."
²⁴For this reason, a man will leave his father and
mother and be united to his wife and they will
become one flesh. ²⁵The man and his wife were
naked and they felt no shame.

43

Although Adam had some sort of relationship with the animals, there is no "suitable helper" for him. So Allah makes a woman from the man and brings her to him. Then we read the first ever recorded human words in Adam's response. "At last...," Adam says - now his loneliness is over. Now he has a suitable helper. Now he has found the one he needs. She is "bone of my bone and flesh of my flesh" – of the same substance as Adam.

The Qur'an comments on this, "It is He (Allah) Who created you from a single person and made his mate of like nature, in order that he might dwell with her (in love)." (al-A'raf 7:189).

Allah institutes marriage. In v.24 there are three aspects of marriage commanded. First a man must leave his parents. This does not mean it is wrong for a married couple to live in the same house as the husband's parents. It does mean that a man's closest relationship is now to his wife. This should be even closer than his relationship to his father and mother. However, he should still honour his parents (al-Taurat, Exodus 20:12).

The second aspect of marriage that Allah commands in v.24 is that the man is to be united to his wife. This speaks of a close and intimate relationship. It is also to be permanent. The Prophet Isa commented on this verse and said, "What Allah has joined together, let no-one separate" (Injil-Matthew 19:6).

Du'a: Allah, thank You for marriage and family life. May we be faithful and loving towards our spouses and other family members.

Day 21

Read Again
Al-Taurat - Genesis 2:20-25

וּלְאָדָ֕ם לֹא־מָצָ֥א עֵ֖זֶר כְּנֶגְדּֽוֹ׃ ²¹ וַיַּפֵּל֩ יְהֹוָ֨ה אֱלֹהִ֤ים ׀
תַּרְדֵּמָה֙ עַל־הָֽאָדָ֖ם וַיִּישָׁ֑ן וַיִּקַּ֗ח אַחַת֙ מִצַּלְעֹתָ֔יו
וַיִּסְגֹּ֥ר בָּשָׂ֖ר תַּחְתֶּֽנָּה׃ ²² וַיִּ֩בֶן֩ יְהֹוָ֨ה אֱלֹהִ֧ים ׀ אֶֽת־
הַצֵּלָ֛ע אֲשֶׁר־לָקַ֥ח מִן־הָֽאָדָ֖ם לְאִשָּׁ֑ה וַיְבִאֶ֖הָ אֶל־
הָֽאָדָֽם׃ ²³ וַיֹּאמֶר֮ הָֽאָדָם֒ זֹ֣את הַפַּ֗עַם עֶ֚צֶם מֵֽעֲצָמַ֔י
וּבָשָׂ֖ר מִבְּשָׂרִ֑י לְזֹאת֙ יִקָּרֵ֣א אִשָּׁ֔ה כִּ֥י מֵאִ֖ישׁ
לֻֽקְחָה־זֹּֽאת׃ ²⁴ עַל־כֵּן֙ יַֽעֲזׇב־אִ֔ישׁ אֶת־אָבִ֖יו וְאֶת־אִמּ֑וֹ
וְדָבַ֣ק בְּאִשְׁתּ֔וֹ וְהָי֖וּ לְבָשָׂ֥ר אֶחָֽד׃ ²⁵ וַיִּֽהְי֤וּ שְׁנֵיהֶם֙
עֲרוּמִּ֔ים הָֽאָדָ֖ם וְאִשְׁתּ֑וֹ וְלֹ֖א יִתְבֹּשָֽׁשׁוּ׃

But for Adam no suitable helper was found. ²¹So the
LORD Allah caused the man to fall into a deep sleep.
While he slept, the LORD Allah took one of his ribs
and closed round it with flesh. ²²And the LORD Allah
built the rib he had taken from the man into a woman
and He brought her to the man. ²³The man said, "At
last, this is bone of my bone and flesh of my flesh. She
will be called 'woman' because she was taken from
man." ²⁴For this reason, a man will leave his father and
mother and be united to his wife and they will become
one flesh. ²⁵The man and his wife were naked and they
felt no shame.

The third aspect of marriage that Allah commands is that they will become one flesh. This speaks of sexual union and it is only to take place within marriage. In this context sex is a beautiful and wonderful thing; a gift from Allah. Adultery and sex before marriage are haraam.

Marriage is a relationship between a man and a woman, so homosexual relationships are also haraam.

Allah did not give these rules to restrict our freedom. They actually provide true freedom to live our lives as our Maker intended. If you buy a machine and then misuse it by going against the maker's instructions, you will not get good use out of the machine. It may break down. It is always wise to obey the maker's instructions. We should obey the instructions of Allah who is our Maker.

Although many prophets and saints took more than one wife, Allah's design at creation was for one man and one wife.

Notice that there is no mention of children here. Children are a great blessing from Allah to any marriage. But the purpose of marriage is not only to have children. Marriage is an end in itself and a blessing from Allah, even if the couple remain childless.

Du'a: "How can those who are young keep their way pure? By living according to Your word. I seek You with all my heart; do not let me stray from your commands." (Zabur 119:9-10)

Day 22

Al-Taurat - Genesis 3:1-3

1 וְהַנָּחָשׁ הָיָה עָרוּם מִכֹּל חַיַּת הַשָּׂדֶה אֲשֶׁר
עָשָׂה יְהוָה אֱלֹהִים וַיֹּאמֶר אֶל־הָאִשָּׁה אַף
כִּי־אָמַר אֱלֹהִים לֹא תֹאכְלוּ מִכֹּל עֵץ הַגָּן:
2 וַתֹּאמֶר הָאִשָּׁה אֶל־הַנָּחָשׁ מִפְּרִי עֵץ־הַגָּן
נֹאכֵל: 3 וּמִפְּרִי הָעֵץ אֲשֶׁר בְּתוֹךְ־הַגָּן אָמַר
אֱלֹהִים לֹא תֹאכְלוּ מִמֶּנּוּ וְלֹא תִגְּעוּ בּוֹ
פֶּן־תְּמֻתוּן:

¹Now the snake was more crafty than all the wild animals the LORD Allah had made. And he said to the woman, "Did Allah really say, 'You must not eat from every tree of the garden'?" ²The woman said to the snake, "We may eat from the fruit of the trees of the garden. ³But Allah said 'You must not eat from the fruit of the tree which is in the middle of the garden, and you must not touch it, or you will die.'"

Snakes were more crafty or clever than other animals. That was the way Allah had made them. This was not bad, but a part of Allah's good creation. Perhaps Adam had noticed this quality when he named the animals.

But this was no ordinary snake. It talked. And there is something wrong here, because it speaks as an enemy of Allah. It creates doubt about Allah's word. Later it goes on to contradict what Allah had said. It seems clear that the enemy of Allah, Iblis, is using this snake as his instrument.

The snake is clever. At first it does not directly contradict Allah's word - that would be too obvious. It just casts doubt on Allah's command: "Did Allah really say…" The snake also creates confusion by quoting Allah as saying, "you must not eat from every tree of the garden."

The woman (Hawwa) answers correctly in line with what Allah commanded in 2:17. However, she does add, "and you must not touch it." Allah had not said that. Is she becoming confused? Does she think that Allah is more strict than He really is?

Du'a: "Lead us not into temptation, but deliver us from the evil one." (Injil-Matthew 6:13)

Day 23

Al-Taurat - Genesis 3:4-6

‎4 וַיֹּאמֶר הַנָּחָשׁ אֶל־הָאִשָּׁה לֹא־מוֹת
‎תְּמֻתוּן: ‎5 כִּי יֹדֵעַ אֱלֹהִים כִּי בְּיוֹם
‎אֲכָלְכֶם מִמֶּנּוּ וְנִפְקְחוּ עֵינֵיכֶם וִהְיִיתֶם
‎כֵּאלֹהִים יֹדְעֵי טוֹב וָרָע: ‎6 וַתֵּרֶא הָאִשָּׁה
‎כִּי טוֹב הָעֵץ לְמַאֲכָל וְכִי תַאֲוָה־הוּא
‎לָעֵינַיִם וְנֶחְמָד הָעֵץ לְהַשְׂכִּיל וַתִּקַּח
‎מִפִּרְיוֹ וַתֹּאכַל וַתִּתֵּן גַּם־לְאִישָׁהּ עִמָּהּ
‎וַיֹּאכַל:

4The snake said to the woman, "You will
not certainly die, 5for Allah knows that
when you eat from it your eyes will
be opened and you will be like Allah,
knowing good and evil." 6The woman saw
that the tree was good for food and that it
was a delight to the eyes and the tree was
desirable for gaining insight, so she took
some of its fruit and she ate it. She also
gave some to her husband who was with
her, and he ate it.

Now the snake contradicts Allah's word: "You will not certainly die..." It then accuses Allah of being selfish: "Allah knows that..." – as if Allah is keeping something good from Hawwa.

The snake promises new experience and wisdom – "Your eyes will be opened." It also promises Hawwa that she "will be like Allah, knowing good and evil." This means that Allah is the One who decides what is good and what is evil. The tree of the knowledge of good and evil represents the moral authority of Allah.

So the snake's message to Hawwa in effect is, "Don't let Allah tell you what you can't do. Don't be under Allah's authority. You be like Allah yourself and decide what's good for you. Appoint yourself judge as to what is good and what is evil."

Hawwa believes the snake instead of Allah. She disobeys Allah, and then Adam follows her. They both rebel against Allah's command. They sin against Allah.

This is actually the sin of *shirk* – of making partners with Allah. The snake told the woman to "be like Allah, knowing good and evil" – in other words, "make yourselves partners with Allah." All sin can be viewed as *shirk* because sin is disobedience and rebellion. It is placing our selves, our will, our desires before Allah. This shows us how serious sin is.

As the Qur'an says, "Man does transgress all bounds, in that he looks upon himself as self-sufficient" (Al-Alaq 96:6-7).

Du'a: Allah, help us to see how terrible and serious disobeying You is.

Day 24

Al-Taurat - Genesis 3:7-8

7 וַתִּפָּקַ֣חְנָה֙ עֵינֵ֣י שְׁנֵיהֶ֔ם וַיֵּ֣דְע֔וּ כִּ֥י
עֵֽירֻמִּ֖ם הֵ֑ם וַֽיִּתְפְּרוּ֙ עֲלֵ֣ה תְאֵנָ֔ה וַיַּעֲשׂ֥וּ
לָהֶ֖ם חֲגֹרֹֽת: 8 וַֽיִּשְׁמְע֞וּ אֶת־ק֨וֹל יְהוָ֧ה
אֱלֹהִ֛ים מִתְהַלֵּ֥ךְ בַּגָּ֖ן לְר֣וּחַ הַיּ֑וֹם
וַיִּתְחַבֵּ֨א הָֽאָדָ֜ם וְאִשְׁתּ֗וֹ מִפְּנֵי֙ יְהוָ֣ה
אֱלֹהִ֔ים בְּת֖וֹךְ עֵ֥ץ הַגָּֽן:

⁷And the eyes of both of them were opened and they knew that they were naked so they sewed fig-leaves together and made coverings for themselves. ⁸Then the man and his wife heard the sound of the LORD Allah going to and fro in the garden in the breeze of the day and they hid themselves from the LORD Allah among the trees in the garden.

The immediate result of Adam and Hawwa's action is that their eyes were opened. That is what the snake had promised - but what a disappointment! All they see is their own nakedness. Sin may promise us happiness, pleasure and fulfilment, but it always leads to disappointment, shame and disaster.

Their new knowledge that they are naked is a sign of their shame. Before, they were naked and at ease with themselves and each other. Now they try to cover up, using fig leaves.

In a similar way the Qur'an says, "when they tasted of the tree, their shame became manifest to them, and they began to sew together the leaves of the garden over their bodies" (al-A'raf 7:22).

But worse is to come. Before their sin they were the crowning glory of Allah's good creation. Allah spoke to them and they were not afraid. They knew Allah and lived under His blessing. But now we find them hiding from Allah.

People still try to hide from Allah. They may do this by ignoring Him, denying that He exists, or even through religion that can be used to suppress and distort the truth about Allah. But it is foolish to try to hide from Allah who is *al-Basir*, the all-seeing.

Du'a: "You have searched me, LORD, and you know me. You know when I sit and when I rise; You perceive my thoughts from afar..." (Zabur 139:1-2)

Day 25

Al-Taurat - Genesis 3:9-12

9 וַיִּקְרָא יְהוָה אֱלֹהִים אֶל־הָאָדָם וַיֹּאמֶר
לוֹ אַיֶּכָּה: 10 וַיֹּאמֶר אֶת־קֹלְךָ שָׁמַעְתִּי בַּגָּן
וָאִירָא כִּי־עֵירֹם אָנֹכִי וָאֵחָבֵא: 11 וַיֹּאמֶר
מִי הִגִּיד לְךָ כִּי עֵירֹם אָתָּה הֲמִן־הָעֵץ
אֲשֶׁר צִוִּיתִיךָ לְבִלְתִּי אֲכָל־מִמֶּנּוּ אָכָלְתָּ:
12 וַיֹּאמֶר הָאָדָם הָאִשָּׁה אֲשֶׁר נָתַתָּה עִמָּדִי
הִוא נָתְנָה־לִּי מִן־הָעֵץ וָאֹכֵל:

[9]The LORD Allah called to the man, "Where are you?" [10]He said, "I heard your voice in the garden and I was afraid because I was naked, so I hid." [11]And He said, "Who told you that you were naked? Have you eaten from the tree from which I commanded you not to eat?" [12]The man said, "The woman You put here with me – she gave me from the tree, and I ate."

Allah does not ask these questions to get information. He is calling Adam to give an account for his action.

Adam's answer in v.10 shows the change that has taken place in the relationship between Allah and Adam. Adam says that he was afraid when he heard Allah's voice. Allah's attitude to Adam has changed. Allah's voice is no longer the voice of blessing, but of anger and grief. Adam also has changed. Now he is afraid of Allah and tries to hide from Him.

Allah's next questions in v.11 give Adam the opportunity to confess his sin – "Yes, I have eaten from the tree You commanded me not to eat." But instead, Adam denies his responsibility. He blames his wife and implies that he did not want her – Allah put her there. This was selfish and cowardly. It must have hurt Hawwa. The relationship between Adam and Hawwa has been spoiled.

Adam also blames Allah for putting the woman there with him; "The woman You put here..." He blames everyone except himself. "A man's folly ruins his life, yet his heart rages against the LORD" (Proverbs 19:3).

Du'a: "Have mercy on me, O Allah, according to Your unfailing love; according to Your great compassion blot out my transgression. Wash away all my iniquity and cleanse me from my sin. For I know my transgressions, and my sin is always before me." (Zabur 51:1-3)

Day 26

Al-Taurat - Genesis 3:13-15

13 וַיֹּאמֶר יְהוָה אֱלֹהִים לָאִשָּׁה מַה־זֹּאת
עָשִׂית וַתֹּאמֶר הָאִשָּׁה הַנָּחָשׁ הִשִּׁיאַנִי
וָאֹכֵל: 14 וַיֹּאמֶר יְהוָה אֱלֹהִים| אֶל־הַנָּחָשׁ
כִּי עָשִׂיתָ זֹּאת אָרוּר אַתָּה מִכָּל־
הַבְּהֵמָה וּמִכֹּל חַיַּת הַשָּׂדֶה עַל־גְּחֹנְךָ
תֵלֵךְ וְעָפָר תֹּאכַל כָּל־יְמֵי חַיֶּיךָ: 15 וְאֵיבָה|
אָשִׁית בֵּינְךָ וּבֵין הָאִשָּׁה וּבֵין זַרְעֲךָ וּבֵין
זַרְעָהּ הוּא יְשׁוּפְךָ רֹאשׁ וְאַתָּה תְּשׁוּפֶנּוּ
עָקֵב:

¹³The LORD Allah said to the woman, "What is this you have done? "The woman said, "The snake deceived me and I ate." ¹⁴The LORD Allah said to the snake, "Because you have done this you are cursed from all livestock and wild animals. You will crawl on your belly and you will eat dust all the days of your life. ¹⁵And I will put enmity between you and the woman and between your offspring and her offspring. He will crush your head, but you will crush his heel."

Hawwa also must answer to Allah for her action. She too tries to shift the blame away from herself.

Allah does not question the snake. He puts a curse on it. Crawling on its belly and eating the dust is a sign of its disgrace and humiliation. Snakes have done this throughout history, but the cursing of the snake is a sign or symbol of the curse of Iblis, whose rebellion against Allah lies behind the snake's action.

Allah also tells the snake that He will place enmity, or hatred between the snake and the woman and between her offspring and his. The offspring of the snake may refer to evil spirits or to wicked human beings.

But then there is a prophecy about a single individual offspring of the woman – "he" (v.15). There will be a terrible conflict in which he will crush the snake's head. He will gain victory over Iblis, destroying him. But there will be a cost; he will suffer - the snake will crush his heel. Here in the middle of disaster, there is a word of hope for humankind - A man will come and destroy Iblis and undo his work.

Du'a: "Out of the depths I cry to You LORD; Lord hear my voice. Let Your ears be attentive to my cry for mercy... I wait for the LORD, my whole being waits, and in His word I put my hope." (Zabur 130:1-2, 5)

Day 27

Al-Taurat - Genesis 3:16

16 אֶל־הָאִשָּׁה אָמַר הַרְבָּה
אַרְבֶּה עִצְּבוֹנֵךְ וְהֵרֹנֵךְ בְּעֶצֶב
תֵּלְדִי בָנִים וְאֶל־אִישֵׁךְ
תְּשׁוּקָתֵךְ וְהוּא יִמְשָׁל־בָּךְ׃

[16]Allah said to the woman, "I will greatly increase your pain in child-bearing. In pain you will give birth to children. Your desire will be for your husband, but he will rule over you."

There are further results and punishments for Adam and Hawwa's sin. Allah announces these to them.

Hawwa's punishment is in relation to her role as mother and wife. Since then every child arrives into the world with pain. Sin affects every human life from its beginning. This is why the Prophet Dawud confesses in the Zabur, "Surely I was sinful at birth, sinful from the time my mother conceived me" (Zabur 51:5). The reason we commit sins is because we have a sinful nature. Sin also affects the relationship between parents and children.

The woman's desire for her husband may be sexual, or it may be the desire to dominate him. Often through history, the husband's rule over the wife has been harsh. Al-Taurat is not saying that such harsh treatment of wives is right. Many of the laws in the Sharia given to Prophet Musa were to protect wives from such harsh treatment. The Injil instructs husbands, "each one of you also must love his wife as he loves himself" and "be considerate as you live with your wives and treat them with respect" (Injil – Ephesians 5:33, 1 Peter 3:7).

Du'a: "Surely I was sinful at birth, sinful from the time my mother conceived me... Create in me a pure heart O Allah." (Zabur 51:5, 10)

Day 28

Al-Taurat - Genesis 3:17-19

¹⁷ וּלְאָדָ֣ם אָמַ֗ר כִּֽי־שָׁמַעְתָּ֮ לְק֣וֹל אִשְׁתֶּךָ֒ וַתֹּ֙אכַל֙ מִן־הָעֵ֔ץ אֲשֶׁ֤ר צִוִּיתִ֙יךָ֙ לֵאמֹ֔ר לֹ֥א תֹאכַ֖ל מִמֶּ֑נּוּ אֲרוּרָ֤ה הָֽאֲדָמָה֙ בַּֽעֲבוּרֶ֔ךָ בְּעִצָּבוֹן֙ תֹּֽאכֲלֶ֔נָּה כֹּ֖ל יְמֵ֥י חַיֶּֽיךָ: ¹⁸ וְק֥וֹץ וְדַרְדַּ֖ר תַּצְמִ֣יחַֽ לָ֑ךְ וְאָכַלְתָּ֖ אֶת־עֵ֥שֶׂב הַשָּׂדֶֽה: ¹⁹ בְּזֵעַ֤ת אַפֶּ֙יךָ֙ תֹּ֣אכַל לֶ֔חֶם עַ֤ד שֽׁוּבְךָ֙ אֶל־הָ֣אֲדָמָ֔ה כִּ֥י מִמֶּ֖נָּה לֻקָּ֑חְתָּ כִּֽי־ עָפָ֣ר אַ֔תָּה וְאֶל־עָפָ֖ר תָּשֽׁוּב:

¹⁷Allah said to the man, "Because you listened to the voice of your wife and ate from the tree from which I commanded you not to eat: cursed is the ground because of you; through painful toil you will eat of it all the days of your life. ¹⁸It will produce thorns and thistles for you and you will eat the plants of the field. ¹⁹By the sweat of your brow you will eat food until you return to the ground, because from it you were taken, for dust you are and to dust you will return."

Adam's punishment is in relation to his role of working the ground. Now the ground is cursed. It produces weeds and pests. There are diseases, droughts, floods and earthquakes. Allah made man to work and that was a blessing. Now his work is difficult and painful. Today also work often causes stress and weariness.

Human life will end in death. Adam will return to the ground from which he was taken. His whole life will be a struggle with the ground, but in the end the man will lose. He will return to dust.

The snake had promised Adam and Hawwa that they would be like Allah when they ate from the tree. That was a lie. They were not and never would be Allah. Here Allah reminds Adam what he really is – he is dust – a creature made of the same material as the earth. Adam and we too should be humble before Allah.

Allah had told Adam that when he ate from the tree of the knowledge of good and evil, he would certainly die (2:17). Now Allah pronounces the death sentence – Adam will return to dust. Allah made humans to live forever. Death is the punishment for sin. It is a curse and a tragedy. We all experience this when we lose a loved one and are separated from them, and also as we approach the day of our own death. We must die because we too are sinners.

Looking back over Genesis 3:7-19, we see a series of broken relationships which are the result and punishment of Adam and Hawwa's sin. There are broken relationships between Allah and humans, between husband and wife, between humans and the environment and even within human beings, with body being ultimately separated from spirit in death.

Du'a: "Lord Allah Almighty, True and just are your judgments." (Injil – Revelation 16:7)

Day 29

Al-Taurat - Genesis 3:20-21

20 וַיִּקְרָ֧א הָֽאָדָ֛ם שֵׁ֥ם אִשְׁתּ֖וֹ חַוָּ֑ה

כִּ֛י הִ֥וא הָֽיְתָ֖ה אֵ֥ם כָּל־חָֽי׃

21 וַיַּ֩עַשׂ֩ יְהֹוָ֨ה אֱלֹהִ֜ים לְאָדָ֧ם

וּלְאִשְׁתּ֛וֹ כָּתְנ֥וֹת ע֖וֹר וַיַּלְבִּשֵֽׁם׃

20Adam named his wife, "Hawwa" because she became the mother of all the living. 21The LORD Allah made garments of skin for Adam and his wife and clothed them.

Adam names his wife "Hawwa." This means "she who gives life." The reason for this name is that she would become the mother of the whole human race. We are all children of Adam and Hawwa. This is why the Qur'an says, "O mankind! Reverence your Guardian-Lord, Who created you from a single person, created of like nature, his mate and from them both scattered (like seeds) countless men and women" (an-Nisa 4:1).

At the end of chapter 2, we read that Adam and Hawwa "were both naked and felt no shame." Their nakedness was a symbol of their innocence. They were open with each other and with Allah – they had nothing to hide.

As soon as they disobeyed Allah, they knew they were naked. They tried to cover up by sewing fig leaves together to make clothing (3:8). As sinners there are things about our lives that we want to hide from others – things that we are ashamed of.

Now Allah makes garments of skin for Adam and Hawwa. Allah confirms their need for covering - Modesty is appropriate for both men and women. But Allah rejects their attempt to provide covering using fig leaves. We cannot cover our sin or make ourselves right with Allah by our own effort. Only Allah can get rid of our shame and sin.

Allah does this by providing clothing from animal skins. Animals had to die in order to provide Adam and Hawwa with coverings that Allah accepted. Sin against Allah is a very serious matter. These animals were the first sacrifices. Later, al-Taurat speaks of the need for sacrifice in order for sins to be forgiven.

Du'a: *"Blessed are those whose transgressions are forgiven, whose sins are covered." (Zabur 32:1)*

Day 30

Al-Taurat - Genesis 3:22-24

²² וַיֹּ֨אמֶר ׀ יְהֹוָ֣ה אֱלֹהִ֗ים הֵ֤ן הָֽאָדָם֙ הָיָה֙
כְּאַחַ֣ד מִמֶּ֔נּוּ לָדַ֖עַת ט֣וֹב וָרָ֑ע וְעַתָּ֣ה ׀ פֶּן־
יִשְׁלַ֣ח יָד֗וֹ וְלָקַח֙ גַּ֚ם מֵעֵ֣ץ הַֽחַיִּ֔ים וְאָכַ֖ל
וָחַ֥י לְעֹלָֽם׃ ²³ וַֽיְשַׁלְּחֵ֛הוּ יְהֹוָ֥ה אֱלֹהִ֖ים מִגַּן־
עֵ֑דֶן לַֽעֲבֹד֙ אֶת־הָ֣אֲדָמָ֔ה אֲשֶׁ֥ר לֻקַּ֖ח
מִשָּֽׁם׃ ²⁴ וַיְגָ֖רֶשׁ אֶת־הָֽאָדָ֑ם וַיַּשְׁכֵּן֩ מִקֶּ֨דֶם
לְגַן־עֵ֜דֶן אֶת־הַכְּרֻבִ֗ים וְאֵ֨ת לַ֤הַט הַחֶ֙רֶב֙
הַמִּתְהַפֶּ֔כֶת לִשְׁמֹ֕ר אֶת־דֶּ֖רֶךְ עֵ֥ץ הַֽחַיִּֽים׃

²²And the LORD Allah said, "Look,
the man has now become like one of us
knowing good and evil. He must not be
allowed to stretch out his hand and
take from the tree of life also and
eat from it and live for ever." ²³So the
LORD Allah sent him out from the
Garden of Eden to work the ground from
which he was taken. ²⁴He drove the man
out and he placed cherubim east of the
Garden of Eden and a flaming sword flashing
forwards and back to guard the way to the
tree of life.

The last result of sin recorded in this chapter is that Allah drives out Adam and Hawwa from the Garden of Eden. By disobeying Allah's command they had rebelled against Allah. They had taken on Allah's role of deciding what was good and evil for themselves. It is in this sense that they have become, in Allah's words, "like one of us, knowing good and evil" (v22).

Allah had created humans to live for ever. The tree of life was a symbol of this. Now they could no longer live for ever – they must die, so Allah bars the way to the tree of life. Allah drives the man out from the garden and places cherubim to guard the way back. Cherubim are heavenly angelic beings. The flaming sword prevents Adam, Hawwa or any of their offspring from going back to the tree of life. If they tried, the sword would kill them.

In the Garden of Eden Adam and Hawwa had lived in the presence of Allah. Now they were expelled from Allah's presence. Allah is *al-Quddus* – the Holy One, who is absolutely pure. Sin always separates us from His presence. Death is the punishment for sin. It includes physical death, but it is more than that. Separation from Allah is spiritual death.

Du'a: "Allah, have mercy on me, a sinner." (Injil-Luke 18:13)

Epilogue

A World Gone Wrong

In Al-Taurat - Genesis 3 we see the origin of the state the world is in today. In this world there are natural disasters such as earthquakes, droughts and floods. There are also accidents, diseases, decay and death. Among humans there is selfishness, greed, hatred, war, cruelty, sexual immorality, idolatry and apathy. And if I know myself and am honest with myself, I know that I am not the person I ought to be.

But Allah did not create the universe like this. When He had made it He declared it all "very good" (1:31). Allah also made humans to rule over the rest of creation. The first humans, Adam and Hawwa were created "very good" but Allah gave them a choice – to obey or disobey Allah.

When Adam and Hawwa disobeyed Allah, the whole of creation, over which they ruled, was affected. They too, and their children, were affected – they became sinners. We can see this very clearly in the fact that Adam and Hawwa's son, Cain (Qabil) murdered his brother, Abel (Habil).

If we are to understand the world in which we live, we must realise that it is not now in the state that Allah originally made it. We live in a world that has gone wrong.

A Visit to the Doctor

This may sound very depressing, but we need to know this. If you go to the doctor with some serious pain, first he needs to diagnose the problem before he can treat you. This is exactly what al-Taurat is doing here. It tells us what the problem is with the world and with the human race – with you and me. Only then does it go on to speak of a treatment and cure.

Healing

Thanks be to Allah, the Holy Kitab does go on to reveal healing, which Allah himself will mercifully give. We even find the first promise of this healing, or salvation, in this chapter. The offspring of the woman would crush the snake's head (3:15). One man would come who would conquer the snake. This theme is developed later on in the Scriptures.

Many years later, Allah promises Prophet Ibrahim, "I will surely bless you… and through your offspring all nations on earth will be blessed." Allah repeated this promise to the Prophets Ishaq and Ya'qub. (al-Taurat – Genesis 22:17-18; 26:4; 28:14)

The Coming King

Later still Allah made a promise to Prophet Dawud, who was king over Isra'il. Allah promised that Dawud's sons would reign for ever. In the Zabur there is a prophecy about a descendent of King Dawud that, "all nations will be blessed through him, and they will call him blessed" (Zabur 72:17).

Over 700 years BC, Allah spoke through the Prophet Isaiah (Shi'ya), predicting that:

> "the Lord Himself will give you a sign:
> the virgin will conceive and give birth to a son…
>
> For to us a child is born, to us a son is given…
> Of the increase of his government and peace there
> will be no end.
> He will reign on Dawud's throne and over his kingdom…
> from that time on and for ever"
> (Isaiah 7:14, 9:6-7).

Around the same time the Prophet Micah prophesied about a ruler who would come from Bayt Lahm (Bethlehem) whose, "greatness will reach to the ends of the earth. And he will be our peace" (Micah 5:2-5).

These and many other prophecies led the children of Isra'il to expect a coming king and deliverer. His title was "al-Masih", which means "the Anointed One."

Anointing was the action of pouring and rubbing oil on the head of a person such as a new prophet, priest, or king. It was a sign that Allah had chosen and given ability and honour to that person for a special task. Al-Masih would be

chosen and anointed by Allah in a unique way for the special work he would
come to do.

Salvation through His Suffering

Allah also revealed that His servant, al-Masih would save people through
suffering. This is suggested when Allah tells the snake, "He will crush your
head, but you will crush his heel." This theme of salvation through al-Masih's
suffering is also developed by later prophets. One example of this is in the
word of Allah which came through the Prophet Isaiah (Shi'ya), around 700
BC:

"Surely he took up our pain and bore our suffering,
    yet we considered him punished by Allah,
stricken by Him and afflicted.
    But he was pierced for our transgressions,
he was crushed for our iniquities;
    the punishment that brought us peace was on him,
and by his wounds we are healed...

By oppression and judgement he was taken away.
    Yet who of his generation protested?
For he was cut off from the land of the living;
    for the transgression of my people he was punished.
He was assigned a grave with the wicked,
    and with the rich in his death,
though he had done no violence,
    nor was any deceit in his mouth." (Isaiah 53:4-5, 8-9).

It was also predicted that after al-Masih's suffering, Allah would exalt and
honour him: "he will be raised, lifted up and highly exalted," and, "After
he has suffered, he will see the light of life and be satisfied" (Isaiah 52:13,
53:11).

Fulfilment

All of these prophecies were fulfilled in the coming of Prophet Isa, who is
al-Masih. The Qur'an attributes the title al-Masih to Isa (al-'Imran 3:45).
The Injil shows us how Isa fulfils all these prophecies and how he brings
peace, healing and salvation for our damaged and dying world.

Read on

This short book has reached its end. Please do read on in the Taurat, Zabur and Injil (also known as The Holy Bible) to find out about Allah's great plan and purpose for this world and for you, if you respond to Him in faith.

Du'a:

"Show me Your ways LORD, teach me Your paths.
Guide me in Your truth and teach me,
for You are Allah my Saviour,
and my hope is in You all day long.
Remember LORD Your great mercy and love,
for they are from of old."
(Zabur 25:4-6)